PROFITABLE
CON
HOW TO PC

S

N

DR. JESSICA HOUSTON

Dedication:

This book is dedicated to my husband,
my daughter, my parents and my siblings.

I love and appreciate you!

This Book Belongs To:

Dr. Jessica Houston

Profitable Conversations
How to Position Yourself for Expansion

Printed in the United States of America

Table of Contents

Foreword

It is very rare an author's introduction provides her readers with such insight and enlightenment. That is typically reserved for the chapters within the book. In, "Profitable Conversations," however, Dr. Jessica Houston, takes her readers on a journey of self- discovery and self-fulfillment before they reach chapter one. She masterfully challenges the status quo as it relates to the meaning of fulfillment and purpose, and she empowers her readers to imagine like they've never imagined before. Once the pages are turned chapter by chapter- she inspires all to avoid doubt, while at the same time giving tangible tools on how to handle disappointment. She ensures her readers know Success is not manifested through some magical formula, nor is it reserved for only a small segment of the population. She brilliantly illustrates how preparation and perseverance can lead to promotion. Each chapter will move readers closer to acquiring more of what they deserve in life. This book is simply the written form of what Dr. Houston shares with audiences nationally and globally, as well as the many individuals she coaches and trains nationally and globally. The exercises and activities provide additional opportunities for dreams, ideas, concepts, and vision to come forth. Once this book is read and re-read and all exercises are completed- not only will readers know they have profited, they will know they have been invested in- with infinite interest and returns which will positively impact generations to come. Make the deposit; invest in yourself by withdrawing doubt while reading this book- and I assure you- you will acquire the tools and information needed to maximize your value both personally and professionally.

Sincerely/I'M POSSIBLE-

Keith L. Brown- "Mr. I'M POSSIBLE-"
Principal Speaker/Consultant/Author/Coach- 2020 Enterprises

Introduction

Introducción

I am so excited to share "Profitable Conversations" with you. I truly believe this book will produce supernatural breakthrough in your life. As you turn each page, you will be stretched and your normal way of thinking will be challenged. It is not by chance that you picked up this book. You had a divine appointment, as you have more untapped potential than you realize. Let me ask you a question. Have you gone "all in" as it relates to achieving your personal and professional goals? It's really easy to blend in, but it takes work to stand out. Listen to me carefully; you were not created to live a mediocre life. Living an adequate life might be sufficient, but it is not fulfilling. It does not matter how much you have accomplished, you know when you feel fulfilled and when you feel as though something is missing. It is important you do not fall into the trap of believing wanting more means you are not grateful for what you already have. You can be grateful and still want more. Once you become more focused, people will try to get you to be less driven. They might even make you feel guilty for wanting more when it looks like you already have a great life. If you are not careful, you will make everyone else happy, but deprive yourself of authentic happiness. In this season, you must ask, "What do I want for me?" Paint that picture and do not let up until you seize what you have envisioned.

I want you to read every chapter with an open mind. Do not skip over the assignments, declarations and activities. Far too often, we read books, take courses and attend conferences, yet we never apply the wisdom we have been given access to. The strategies shared will work if you implement them. How can I be so confident? I am confident, because what I am sharing is based upon personal experience. I have encountered trials, disappointments and setbacks that I want you to avoid. As I travel the world, people look at me and they see a semi-polished product. They see me walking in my purpose and impacting lives. However, they never saw the tears, the worry and the frustration I had to break through. I now walk in confidence and know my value, but it took years for me to get here. It took years of processing and overcoming. I could not understand why I had to go through so much when I was in the middle of my wilderness. But in retrospect, had I not experienced a wilderness of my own, I would not be in a position to coach you. By reading this book, you get the benefit of reaching your destination quicker. You also get to avoid many of the rough patches I experienced. You should be celebrating right now, as you literally have access to classified insight. It's like going into a battle with your opponent's battle plan in your hand.

Do not take what you learn lightly. This book is written by a woman who never would have imagined being where she is today. I was born with club feet and had to have surgery on both of my ankles. I was diagnosed with a rare form of meningitis and the doctors were not sure if I would make it. I overcame severe low self-confidence, depression and a suicide attempt. I can go on and on about the trauma I have experienced. The great news is my experiences were not in vain. Now, let's get ready to position you for the expansion you have been seeking. I want you to applaud your colleagues when they win, but I also want you to recognize you are a winner too. You have untapped brilliance within you and I am looking forward to pulling it out. You have ideas that must be released into the marketplace. You have dreams you have placed on the backburner, but your days of slow progress are over. It is time for you to accelerate. Fasten your seatbelt and enjoy the ride!

CHAPTER 1

Avoiding the Pitfall of Doubt

At some point, every one of us has fallen into the pitfall of doubt. At this moment, you might be wondering, why I am calling doubt a pitfall. Well, a pitfall is a hidden danger or difficulty. One of the greatest dangers associated with doubt is that most people never recognize the magnitude of impact that doubt carries. Unfortunately, for many people, doubt has become a way of life. We might talk about faith and positive thinking, but the real test comes when we enter an extremely challenging situation. Yes, we might generally believe that our situation will improve. However, there can be moments when our situation seems dismal. During these moments a seed of doubt can be planted. Although it is a thought that simply crossed your mind, if it is not addressed, it can lure you into a pitfall of doubt. As the manager of your thoughts and emotions, you have the authority to prevent doubt from taking up residence in your mind. Doubt is a breakthrough blocker. Think about it, your victory begins in your mind. So, if you have lost the battle in your mind, you have lost the battle. Period.

Can I just talk with you like we are sitting down at a local coffee shop having a casual conversation? I hope so, because I don't believe in sugarcoating anything. I keep it real and I expect the same thing in return. The first time I was told that I am very direct, I saw it as a deficit. I thought, well, I don't want to hurt anyone's feelings. This is true, I am one of the nicest people you will ever meet. But it is very difficult for me to not be honest with someone who is heading down the wrong path. Just this week, I was told that I am a "matter of fact" kind of person. I kind of let it marinate and then I said to myself: "I am and I'm okay with that." Now, I have finally reached a place where I don't wonder what is wrong with me when people say I am very direct. We are all unique and that is a good thing. I let my coaching/consulting clients know my coaching style ahead of time. They know that I love them enough to tell them the truth. This discovery has actually helped me clarify my coaching style and whom I am called to serve. There are individuals who do not handle feedback well. So, they prefer to work with people who will tell them what they want to hear. That is fine, but I recognize that we would not be a great fit.

Now, back to this topic of doubt. Whenever you find yourself doubting your gifts, abilities, talents, and skills, remember that doubt repels, but belief attracts. If you doubt you will ever find a good husband/wife, you probably won't. With life, we ultimately receive what we expect to receive. Often, doubt is an automatic response to distressing news. What I'd like to do is help you become familiar with a few of the common ways that doubt can impact your frame of mind. I am also excited to teach you what you can do to protect your progress. Are you ready? I hope so. Let's go!

First You Must Guard Your Ears

When going through a storm or seeking to expand your territory, you must be intentional about guarding your ears. You must view this principle as your duty. If you ignore it, you will allow unqualified people to speak into your life. I have a question for you, who are you listening to? Please, listen closely. Everyone is NOT authorized to be in your ear. Never be so desperate for help you will take advice and guidance from someone without checking their track record. It is also imperative you look at how the person desiring to advise you is living. You may wonder why this is so important. Often, we listen to people just to be nice and we figure it would be rude to stop them. However, your ear is the gateway to your mind. I will not discuss mindset right now, but we will go more in depth about the power of your mind later. When you give someone your ear, you give them your time, your energy and an opportunity to either build you up or tear you down. You give them intimate access to you, which can become dangerous. Think about it, the person talking to you has the power to control your emotions. They can upset you, offend you, encourage you or discourage you.

What I have noticed is that some of the very people trying to guide you, can't even guide themselves. Could it be that they are trying to discourage you from pursuing your dream, because they are afraid that you will outgrow them? Could it be that they are secretly competing with you? Take notice of the people who tell you that your vision is too big. Also, guard your ears against listening to drama and negativity. You cannot grow if you are connected to people who get excited about gossip and negativity. Someone always telling you what someone has said negatively about you can't want to see you happy. Guard your ears and take charge of your destiny.

Second, Guard Your Thoughts

Besides guarding your ears, you must also guard your thoughts. Your mind is very susceptible to attack because our brains are constantly in motion. Even while we are sleeping our brains are active. According to the Cleveland Wellness

Clinic we have between 35 and 48 thoughts per minute and on average about 80 percent of our habitual thoughts are negative. It has been scientifically proven that our brains are hard-wired to focus more on the negative than the positive. This can actually be helpful for picking up on impending danger or harm. However, far too often negative thoughts become so consuming that we often disregard what is going well in our lives.

When a negative thought enters your mind, it must be cast down immediately. You must recognize when your thoughts are inaccurate. Also realize that negative thoughts do not deserve to take up residence in your mind. If you do not monitor and control your thoughts, they will weigh you down and keep you in bondage. If you do not remember anything else, remember that your thoughts are powerful. They can either help you or hinder you. However, the good news is that you can choose which thoughts you accept and which thoughts you must cast down.

Third, Guard Your Words

Do you realize how powerful your words are? This is an often-overlooked pitfall. We get into a habit of speaking our thoughts and if you remember, most of our thoughts are negative and must be revamped. Your words are just as important as your thoughts. In reality, they are weapons that can work for you or against you. As a little girl, I can remember my mom telling me that my mouth can get me in a lot of trouble. I brushed those words off because I thought I knew everything. However, I eventually had to admit that she was right.

Whenever you speak something negative about yourself, someone else, or your situation, do 3 things. First, recognize that what you just uttered is negative. From there, you should revoke those words. Yes, even if you didn't really mean what you said. Something stated in anger is still a seed spoken into the atmosphere. Our words have so much more power than most people realize. This is why revoking negative words spoken is only the second step. The final step involves replacing the negative declaration with something positive. For example, 'I will never get out of this debt' should be revoked and replaced with 'I will be debt free.'

It is possible to become so accustomed to negative self-talk that you fail to recognize how often you are speaking against what you actually want. Hey, I'm right there with you. I must manage my thoughts and words daily. Think about it, if you say something repeatedly, you believe it and it becomes a self-fulfilling prophecy. So, instead of complaining and declaring your problems, speak life into your situation. Stop what you are doing right now and tell God 'thank you.' Have a praise party instead of having a pity party. Only speak what you desire to take place.

My challenge to you is this, speak what you desire and not what you fear. Speak the promises of God out loud daily. It's not enough to just read them or think them. Do not be deceived by what you see. Do not be deceived by what you feel. Remember, there is power in the spoken word. Can I count on you to only speak victory?

Finally, Activate Your Faith

Your next level will require radical faith. Be mindful of what you are listening to, thinking and/or speaking. The only question to ask is: does this line up with the word of God? Faith is the substance of things hoped for and the evidence of things not seen (Hebrews 11:1). Remember, NOTHING is too hard for God. God wants you to be freed from anything that drains or disturbs you, but your faith activates his promise!

Some days you will wonder if God hears your cries in the dark. Guess what. He's right there with you. Even when it feels like he is far away, he is paving the way, guiding you through the growth process step by step. Now, you would rather sprint or better yet fly to your destination, but God is an orderly God. His timing rarely coincides with our timing, but it is always perfect. If you try to jump ahead of God, you will prolong the process and you may have to start over from scratch. There a people that he wants you to meet and places he desires for you to go. However, he knows that you must be adequately prepared for what he's planning to bring you into.

Do not despise your season of preparation. It's easier said than done, but God wants to know if you will still serve him and praise him, even when things are not going your way. The bible talks about the sacrifice of praise. It is during those moments of brokenness that you must be determined to maintain your faith. Doubt, impatience, and fear are distractions. Pursue peace and activate your faith. God has a plan for your life, so please don't forfeit it by throwing in the towel.

CHAPTER 2

Walking in Your Purpose

Walking in
Your Purpose

P urpose is a widely discussed topic, but it is often covered on a basic level. You may have heard someone say that the two most important days of your life are the day you were born and the day you discovered why you were born. In this chapter, I want you to understand that discovering your purpose is a process. For this reason, it can be frustrating when you are searching for a specific formula. There is not anything wrong with reading an article, completing a worksheet or taking an online assessment. It is just important that you recognize these as tools and not a roadmap to discovering your purpose. Now you might be thinking, isn't this chapter about walking in your purpose? Yes, it is, but I want to make sure that you are not just taking a path that someone has recommended for you. I want you to be intentional about the path you choose for your life. Far too many people are on jobs they hate, and it is depleting their joy.

We live in a society where we desire and expect immediate answers, but I am urging you to not put too much pressure on yourself. Discovering your purpose is more than simply identifying your gifts, talents, and skills. Your life assignment is major, so you do not want to rush the self-discovery process. Your purpose is the reason you were created. It is easy to get the impression that your career or your profession is your purpose. However, in most cases your purpose and your career are not the same. Your purpose is not a specific destination. It actually evolves and expands based upon your level of growth. This is why walking in your purpose is exciting, yet uncomfortable. Just when you get to the place where you feel like you've got it, you will probably be thrown a curve ball. You will be challenged to do something different.

At first, you will be a little anxious and maybe even afraid. However, if you are willing to be stretched, you will allow yourself to see how talented and brilliant you are.

Contrary to popular belief, walking in your purpose requires courage. You will find that you become a different person as you begin the journey of walking in your purpose. As seasons change, people will enter your life and people will leave your life. People may wonder why you have become less interested in activities not connected to your purpose, such as (television, hanging out, going to parties, etc.). Now, this is not to say that you will not have fun. It just means you will become more selective about how you spend your time. If you are serious about accomplishing anything extraordinary, you must learn how to manage your time wisely. We will talk more about this in Chapter 3. Everyone will not be happy with the new and improved you. Do not be surprised if some people who you have been close to for years slowly pull away. People enter and leave our lives for a reason. It can be frustrating, even more so, when you do not understand what is happening.

I have learned not to get too comfortable with my life assignments because purpose is always evolving. I will take a moment to give you a little background about how I transitioned into my new normal. After earning my MSW (Master in Social Work), I was certain that my purpose was to be a social worker. I had the training, the certification, the skill and I enjoyed helping others. I was very excited when I landed my first school social work position. I was very comfortable in my position. I could do school social work with minimal effort. I recognized this about three years before I left my position, but I had heard repeatedly that people retire in school social work positions. So, I told myself that I needed to just be grateful that I was blessed to have such a great position.

However, as much as I tried to fool myself, I no longer felt fulfilled. My growth and excitement as it related to my position hit a plateau. I managed a grant for three years and I found that fascinating, but once it ended, I went right back to feeling as though something was missing. As time passed, feelings of discontent became stronger. Although I was smiling on the outside, I felt like something was missing. I felt like I was supposed to be doing something else, but I could not figure out what that "something else" was. So, I researched franchises and I thought about opening a restaurant. It sounded interesting, but deep within my soul, I knew that I had no passion for owning a restaurant.

The void weighed on me for a while and I became determined to figure out my next move. I didn't give up. I just kept thinking about and researching various business ventures. I even took two online assessments. What puzzled me was that the assessments always put me back in social work, counseling or something similar. Well, one day I realized that I did not have to abandon my skills. It was like a light bulb went off and I got it. It was just time for me to utilize my skills in a different way. From this point, God impressed upon me to write my first book titled: Women's Secrets: It's Time to Stop Suffering in Silence. I wrote my first book, not because I wanted to, but because I knew that I was commissioned to write it.

God simply told me to write a book. That was the first step. Honestly, I really didn't know where I would go from there, but God knew. I leaned on him for guidance and there were many days of frustration. Social work was my comfort zone, but because of my obedience, I was being stretched way more than I intended to be stretched. So, before moving on, I will say this: do not look to see or understand God's plan for your life in totality. He WILL NOT reveal his entire plan at once. You just must be willing to trust him. Are you willing to surrender your will to God's will and be obedient when he asks you to do something? Now, before you answer, make sure that you are all in. I can tell you from experience that much of what God asks you to do will seem strange and often it will scare you. However, if you do not yield to what he is asking you to do, you will only slow your progress.

Get Out Of Your Comfort Zone

My first speaking engagement took place while I was still a school social worker. I had just published my book and a co-worker asked if I would come to her home and speak to a group of women. There were about 15 women there. I spoke and I sold 20 books. I actually spoke at her house twice for two groups of women.

My first time speaking in front of a large group was when I served as co-chair for the school social worker's organization (GA). I thought that my heart would pound its way out of my chest. The microphone was shaking in my hand, but I did it.

As I continue to walk in my divine purpose, I often think about the fact that all of this started with me responding to a nudge from God. I could have stayed within my norm and retired as a school social worker. My colleagues thought I had lost my mind when I left the position. When I was hired, I was told there were over 100 applicants for the position I was hired for. Great pay, great benefits and a lot of paid time off. So, this caused me to question myself. Why aren't you content? I didn't know why then, but I understand why now. It was because the plan I had for my life was too small. Ultimately, it was up to me to step out of my comfort zone and into my destiny.

When people see me speaking at prestigious organizations and international conferences, they see the result of my efforts. However, they are not aware of what it took for me to get there. Sometimes, I lost money. Sometimes, I arrived at an event where I was told there would be 50 people, but there were actually only 8 people in the audience. This did not happen just once or twice; it happened several times. If I can be honest, I was disappointed. In a few instances, I had agreed to speak for free in exchange for selling my products. Now, had this happened while I was still working a full-time job it would not have been a big deal. However, when your business is your primary income generator, these experiences can send you into despair. They can make you question whether you should just go back to work. Working a job is much easier. You have less responsibility and you can count on your check being deposited at the end of each pay period. Entrepreneurship is not for the faint at heart. You must have tenacity, commitment and determination. Yes, it would have been easier to get a job. But, I knew that even with the highs and lows of entrepreneurship, going back to a full-time job was not an option. God had clearly outlined my path. I remember hearing Joyce Meyer say, "We live life forward, but understand it backwards." Her statement is true. In retrospect, I realize that God was humbling me. God was also testing me to see if I was committed. He wanted to know if I was in this for the money and the popularity or if I was truly concerned about transforming lives.

Your Choices Shape Destiny

I love helping my clients gain clarity about what they REALLY want. Far too often, women, in particular, choose their path based upon what will make others happy. They pull back because they do not want to appear mean or selfish. They say well, this is just not the right time. As soon as (insert excuse) is taken care of, I will focus on me. Ok, coaching moment: you will always have a reason to postpone your dream. There will always be someone who needs you – A LOT. It all comes down to whether or not you are going to finally take yourself off of the backburner.

By not pursuing what you want, you ultimately settle for what you don't want. Do you know that greater is calling you? Do you know that you have gifts, talents, and skills you have not even tapped into yet? Maybe you have let several six or seven-figure ideas slip away. We do it all the time. We think about it, we get excited and then suddenly, we think of a dozen reasons it won't work. What if you consciously decided to follow through on just one of your ideas?

What might happen if you pushed through the doubt and the fear? I have found that women, in particular, will push everyone around them forward, yet they are standing still.

They are encouraging everyone else to pursue their dreams, yet they are going to a job every day they despise. Today, I'm challenging you to make the difficult choices. I do not recommend that you abruptly quit your job. However, I do recommend that you go through the process of discovering what would excite you about getting out of bed every morning. Don't worry about the what ifs. Don't even worry about what you are lacking. Simply decide to discover and utilize every gift that has been placed inside of you. If you have been thinking there has to be more in life, you are right. Sometimes, you just need someone in your corner who can help you push past the doubts holding you back. Discovering and walking in your purpose will allow you to be someone's answered prayer. But it doesn't stop there you will literally feel like you just did CPR on your life!

CHAPTER 3

Your "YES" is Valuable

What have you been saying yes to over the last six months to one year? Do you weigh your return on investment before saying yes to the requests of friends, family, colleagues, and others? Have your decisions moved you closer to your goals or have they taken you off course? Take a moment and respond to the opening questions truthfully. Your responses will inevitably reveal whether you have been valuing your yes. This chapter is to help you think critically about your method of decision-making. Decision-making is a process. Often, however, we feel pressured and make decisions on the spot. Now, sometimes, time really is of the essence. But you can ask the person seeking your time, energy, ideas and even your money to give you some time to process their request. If you are not comfortable asking them for time to think about it, simply state you need to review your other commitments before making a new commitment. If you know in your gut that saying yes to the offer in front of you will send you into a state of overwhelm, be upfront and honest. You never want to overextend yourself physically, emotionally, or financially. You cannot be everything to everyone. To maintain your peace and sanity, you must set limits. You are ultimately responsible for how you manage your time. When you finish reading this chapter, you should walk away knowing that your yes is valuable. If you have ever been in an audience where I was the speaker, then you know how much I enjoy call and response. So, take a moment and pretend I am directly in front of you. Ok, now repeat after me My Yes Is Valuable! Guess what, you are correct. Even the simplest yes can affect the trajectory of your destiny. This is why you must process your requests in a different way. Even those situations that seem like a huge opportunity must be evaluated.

Decision Making

Decision-making in its simplest form is the act of making a choice. Most of our daily choices are not complicated. However, each and every one of us have found ourselves in a place where we had to make a tough decision. You might be asking yourself, do I remain in this unhealthy relationship? Do I go for the promotion? Is it time for a career change? Do I admit that I am struggling with addiction or depression? When confronted with a tough decision you likely weigh the advantages against the disadvantages. You might even ask a trusted confidant their opinion. However, the final decision should be yours and yours alone. While others mean well, you are the person who must live with the decisions you make.

Whenever you are pondering a decision, it is imperative that you consider your emotional state. We were given emotions for a reason. They are very helpful. However, they can also blur our vision. You might be wondering well what do emotions have to do with valuing my yes? Great question by the way. Your emotions have a lot to do with valuing your yes. So, let's delve a little deeper into the importance of emotional intelligence. You must always be aware of emotions like excitement, fear, guilt, anger, sadness, and so forth. I recommend that you never make a major decision while you are in a highly emotional state. When I say major, I mean a decision that will significantly affect your time, finances, health and/or relationships. It is possible to make an emotional decision and not even realize it. When your feelings and emotions are running rampant, you rarely think to ask critical questions. Consequently, you might say yes to something that you would have normally said no to. If you have little time, I recommend that you at least take a few minutes to figure out how this new request or perceived opportunity (venture, partnership, relationship) will affect your current schedule and/or obligations.

Being offered a new opportunity can be exciting. Most of us welcome the emotion of excitement and we should. However, understand that excitement can lessen your ability to make a logical decision. For example, you can be so excited that you breeze through the contract and miss a key clause. I'm not saying you should tone down your excitement. I am recommending that you do not make a decision during the peak of your excitement. Based upon personal experience, I can attest that you can get so emotional that your feelings overshadow the truth. In that moment, you cannot see past your feelings. You might have butterflies in your stomach. You might drift off into dreamland. You might even blurt out "yes, I would love to" without even realizing it. Unfortunately, you can get so wrapped up in your emotions and feelings you ignore clear warning signs. This is why you can probably look back on past challenges and wonder how everyone around you saw what you could not see. Here is your answer: you could not see clearly because you were being led by your emotions. Once you shut your emotions down, your spiritual discernment will kick in and reveal what your emotions would not allow you to see. Let's be honest, we have all made an emotional decision before. I hope after reading this chapter, you will be prompted to weigh the pros and cons of your decisions.

When I started getting invitations to speak, write articles and be interviewed, I was elated. I was so happy to receive an invitation I would typically say yes without even taking a moment to think about what I was saying yes to. Sometimes my yes would lead to a new opportunity, but most times my time and energy resulted in little or no return on my investment. Eventually, I got to a point where I was busy all the time. I was doing a lot of things, but I was not getting the results that my efforts deserved. So, while those on the receiving end were happy, I was deeply frustrated. In retrospect, I was frustrated because I was not being intentional. I was taking action, but I was not taking the right actions. Have you ever experienced this? There is a huge difference between being busy and being productive. So, from today forward, I need you (in my coaching voice) to carefully weigh your invitations. What is the end result you are looking for? You must always begin with the end in mind.

Time Management

As you have probably recognized by now, I love asking questions. As a coach, asking the right questions can produce tremendous breakthroughs. So, as we delve into time management, ponder this question: How often do I say "Yes" when I really want to say "No"? Time is a gift and it is not just any gift; it is a precious gift. During my youth, I did not recognize the value of my time and it never crossed my mind that once your time has been spent, you cannot get it back. Now that I understand that time is my most precious resource, I am careful not to waste it. I am very intentional about my time and I surround myself with people who value my time. I no longer allow others to determine how I will utilize my time. This is an important teaching moment for you. Allow no one to guilt you out of your time. Once you take control over your time, you will see an increase in your productivity.

Now, to effectively manage your time, you must become comfortable saying NO. Do you see how this aligns with valuing your yes? Scarcity results from infrequency. This means that utilizing the word "NO" actually increases the value of your YES. Is that powerful or what? Your goal should be to get to a place where people recognize that you do not invest in meaningless battles or activities. Use discretion when giving people access to your time and attention!

There is no way you can do everything that you want to do AND everything that everyone else wants you to do. If you desire to be a wealth generator, you must understand just how valuable your time is. When I recognized the value of my time, I was still afraid to say no, because I wanted to be considered nice. I didn't want to let anyone else down, but I ultimately let myself down. Because I am a helper and a giver, I never wanted to be perceived as selfish. So instead of saying no, I would commit to things I really did not want to commit to. I did not realize that I was still a helper and a giver, even if I periodically was not available to help those close to me. I recommend that you ask yourself some questions, before agreeing to any task (not employer related) that you are being asked to do. There are many questions you can ask, but these are a few to think about.

1. Do I really want to do this? Make sure that you are not agreeing out of guilt or fear of hurting the other person's feelings.
2. Does this benefit me, my family or a cause that I'm passionate about?
3. Does this person always ask me for favors but rarely asks how he/she can support what I'm doing?
4. Do I have time to do this?
5. Will adding another project or task send me into a state of anxiety or overwhelm?

Even if you enjoy helping others (like me), there will be times when, you must exercise your right to Say No. High achievers prioritize and structure their days. You must set boundaries and let those close to you know that your success is contingent upon your productivity. So as your coach, I am challenging you to nurture and protect your vision. Your time is valuable, and it should never be wasted. When you are gifted, people will pull on you, but ultimately, you are responsible for managing you.

Defeating the Peril of Impatience

It's better to try and miss the mark than to look back and wonder what would have happened if you had pursued what you REALLY wanted. Have you ever allowed fear and impatience to deprive you of what you deserve? I know I have. I had my idea of how long it should take for me to get married, have children, earn a certain salary, etc. I have always been a goal getter and that's great. But I have also had the tendency to be hard on myself and that is not good. Yes, stretch yourself, but you must also learn not to beat yourself up when you miss the mark. I say "when" because we all miss the mark at times. Missing the mark can be frustrating, but it should be viewed as an opportunity to learn something new and as an opportunity to improve your strategy. There is no greater teacher than personal experience.

When you sow a seed, you must cultivate it, nurture it and protect it. You must give your seed time to blossom. Don't plant a seed (idea/want/desire) and then abandon it out of frustration. You should never abandon your desire, just because it did not produce within the time frame you have set. Often, we downsize our dream or settle for good enough. When you are in a season of waiting, mediocre offers might appeal to you. However, I urge you to hold out for the desires of your heart. Do not be lured by impatience. Impatience can lure you into making a poor decision. Impatience leads to desperation, desperation leads to poor decision-making, and poor decision-making ultimately leads to regret.

Trust me. I know that it's not easy to be patient. But I also know that getting what you truly deserve will be worth the wait. You might say, well it's not what I want, but it's better than waiting. Far too often the end result is settling for mediocre relationships, jobs, friends, and so forth. But God is saying son/daughter will you just hold out until I open the door, until I send the spouse, until I send the right opportunity? If you do, I promise I will blow your mind. Teaching Moment: Your impatience can cause you to settle and forfeit what God intends for you to have. When you feel as though you are not making any progress, I need you to stop and think about how far you've come. I need you to start a victory journal. This will be a journal you can go back to whenever doubt creeps in.

Sometimes, you must remind yourself of God's track record. Overachievers are wired to downplay victories and magnify defeats. This tracking process of thinking will lock you into a pattern of feeling like you are a total failure, when, in fact, you are not even close to being a failure. Every step counts. Every small victory counts. So, instead of focusing on what is missing, celebrate how far you have come. I will bet there are victories you have forgotten about.

Please do not think yourself into a state of anxiety. You are being prepared for something greater, you just must change your perception of your situation. Again, don't be quick to say "Yes" because some agreements are easy to get into, but difficult to get out of. It doesn't matter what everyone else seems to be doing. You were not created to settle. Set high standards as it relates to your career, business, priorities, relationships and so forth. In my early 20s my main selection criteria for dating was "How does he look? Does he dress well? Is he taller than me when I'm wearing heels?" Now, I recognize that it's more important that you check their character, their ambition and their work ethic. I hope you realize that valuing your yes applies to relationships too.

You Deserve the Best

You probably have a general idea of what you would like your life to look like in 5 years. However, have you ever taken the time to think about what you want in detail? Have you evaluated every aspect of your life? What goals do you have related to your relationships, career, finances, health and spirituality? If you haven't taken the time to write down your ideal future and how you plan to get there, I challenge you to do it sooner rather than later. It's easy to evaluate the attitude, behavior and/or habits of someone else. However, we must conduct an honest evaluation of ourselves. As you brainstorm what you really want, you may realize that you are behind schedule or not heading in the right direction. Don't use this assessment as an opportunity to have a pity party or beat yourself up. Instead, use this assessment to create a solid strategy. Once you recognize what has been holding you back, you can take action steps that will get you closer to your desired destination. What important action can you take today? Not next week, but today. Once you decide, you must commit to making it happen.

Every decision should align with what you value and what you desire. This is why you must know from the start what you really want. Distractions are all around us. So, if we are not careful, we can pursue a path we were never intended to pursue. Someone can come along and convince you to buy into their dream. Don't get me wrong it's great to support others. But you also have a mandate. You also have a purpose. You don't want to wake up one morning and wonder why you are not anywhere near where you could have been if you had pursued the path created for you. If you don't know what you want, you are likely to accept whatever you are offered. Sometimes opportunists will see in you what you don't see, and they will take advantage of your kindness.

There will be people in a position to help you and connect you with life changing opportunities, yet they will choose not to help you. If you are not careful, you will become so engulfed in who is not supporting you, that you slow or even halt your progress. Being selective is important, because you should not partner with everyone who "seems" like a great partner. There will likely be individuals who ask you for time and resources they are not willing to reciprocate. These are the individuals who only call you when they need something. Once you know who is draining you, you have a decision to make. Will you continue to allow people to take advantage of your kindness? If you do not remember anything that I have shared, remember that you must be very intentional about how you invest your time and energy. Ok, last question of this chapter. Do you promise to be selective about who and what gets a yes from you? This is not you making a promise to me. Instead, this is you making a promise to you.

CHAPTER 4

Handling Disappointment

Disappointment is the feeling that bubbles up in response to an unfulfilled hope or expectation. Some disappointments are minor and we get past them relatively quickly. However, when major disappointments occur, it takes more effort to bounce back. Although disappointment is a natural response, we have control over how we respond to it. There are many ways to handle disappointment and I will cover several in this chapter. However, I would like for you to take a moment to reflect upon how you typically respond to disappointment and frustration. Do you talk it out? Do you hold it in? Do you become angry? Do you panic? Are you consumed with feelings of anxiety or hopelessness? It is imperative you are aware of how you respond to disappointment because you cannot fix a leak you are not aware of. Often, we respond out of mere habit. This is why I recommend that you stop to reflect upon and answer the questions before moving on. In doing so, you can take note of the emotional triggers that produce feelings of fear, sadness, anxiety and even anger.

My goal is to help you discover and overcome the thought patterns that have prevented you from preserving your peace, your joy, your happiness, and your energy. For example, worry is a thought pattern that drains you. If you are not careful, you can become so frustrated that you diminish your productivity. Often, your mind becomes consumed with uncertainty about your future and it becomes difficult to focus on simple tasks. Likewise, you also begin to gradually lose the passion and excitement you started with. You want everything to run smoothly. No one looks forward to receiving a rejection letter or experiencing an unexpected setback. However, life happens and there are situations that we cannot control. When you experience disappointment, your response matters. I'm not saying you can't acknowledge that you are disappointed. I want you to be honest about your feelings because attempting to suppress your disappointment will only postpone the healing process. We all encounter losses and rejection. We all encounter challenges and should be fighting for our joy and our peace daily. You are not an imposter just because you experienced a meltdown. You are still qualified to coach, teach and lead even if you have moments of sadness. You are not a superhero, so remove your cape and give yourself permission to be human.

There is not anything wrong with setting the bar high but don't let the overachiever in you cause you to sink into a state of depression. On the surface, perfection seems like a great quality. But at the root of perfectionism is fear. Fear of failure, fear of making a mistake, fear of being laughed at, fear of people discovering that you don't have it all together. News Flash: Nobody has it all together. We all have areas we can improve in. Let me help you, if you are breathing, you have not reached your peak. Yes, sometimes, you miss the mark. Yes, sometimes, you make a poor decision. Yes, sometimes, you respond so it escalates the situation instead of de-escalating it. If you have been struggling with perfectionism, I am challenging you to give yourself permission to be imperfect. Repeat after me (Your Name) you have permission to be imperfect. (Your Name) I forgive you for _____. Write this down and repeat it as many times as you need to. Your emotional freedom begins when you declare that you are free.

Persisting Beyond Your Setback

A common thread among those who are successful is persistence. People afraid to fail never get started and therefore they never can succeed. Embracing the possibility of failure can be difficult. However, if you do not receive the outcome you anticipated, understand that success does not happen overnight. Often, it looks like others achieved success quickly, when in reality they have endured many setbacks and disappointments. They may never share their journey with you, but if you ask any successful person if their journey was easy, they can probably talk for hours about what they had to overcome to get where they are right now. You can't compare your starting point to another person's peak. Some people whom you admire went through years of preparation and multiple failures. When you fall short of your goal, this indicates that your strategy must be revised.

Persisting beyond failure means you must acknowledge the failure, analyze what did not work and intentionally decide to move forward. Remaining in defeat mode will not improve your chances of moving forward. When you focus on the problem and not the solution, you will not be productive. You must remember why you pursued your vision in the first place. How strong is your why? If it's not strong enough, you won't be able to keep going when you run into challenges or tough times. Those who succeed are not fearless, they had to show up, even when they were afraid. They had to go after opportunities that seemed scary. At some point, they probably wondered if they were good enough, smart enough or talented enough to reach the goals they had set. What separates high achievers from their mediocre colleagues is their decision not to succumb to their fears. Remember, a past failure does not determine your future outcome. You cannot go back and change what has already occurred. However, you have the power to create an amazing future. Failure is only permanent if you quit. As you continue to press towards your goals, never allow your disappointments to discourage you, allow them to fuel you!!

Restructuring Your Response

Initially, I asked you how you respond to disappointment and frustration. As you grow into the person you are destined to become, you must learn how to discipline your response. You might be thinking, well how do I discipline my response? Well, first understand that your reactions are grounded in your habits. So, if you typically respond by complaining, having a pity party, getting angry or by becoming self-critical, there is a good chance that you have been doing this (without realizing it) for a long time. The great news is that you can manage your emotions and your response.

Before you panic, recognize that a disappointment is not the end of the world. Our brains tend to extremize, which basically means that our perception of our situation can make our challenge to appear much worse than it actually is. Your perception can cause you to view your situation as all or nothing. For example, if you just experienced a breakup, your mind might say I will never find someone who will be faithful. As you look over your finances, you might feel as though you will never get out of debt. You may make a simple mistake and your mind will make you feel as though you have ruined your career. These are just a few examples of how your response can make you feel worse instead of uplifting and empowering you. What if you changed your response? What if you took a deep breath and consciously decided to invest your energy in figuring out your next best step?

A few questions you can ask yourself are: What needs to be revised? What worked? What didn't work? What lessons did I learn? Most times our challenges are not as bad as our minds have made them out to be. It's all about your perception and what you choose to believe about your situation. Whenever you feel discouraged, I'm challenging you to begin to strategize instead of complaining or having a pity party. If your words or thoughts are not uplifting, you must get rid of them. Fear, disappointment, frustration, and rejection are all components of the growth process. So, if you are looking to elevate your life, your mind, your career and/or your brand, decide that you WILL NOT allow the growth process to break you. Dwelling on disappointment causes you to doubt the promises you have been given. Although we perceive success as a straight path, it is really a winding road constantly under construction. There will be detours, but you must revise your strategy and keep pressing.

If you have not been hearing "No," this indicates that you have not been seeking new opportunities. Do not let your fear of hearing "No" discourage you. Every "No" brings you one step closer to your "YES." Everyone is not supposed to say yes to you. Your products, dreams, interests, and services will not resonate with everyone. However, there are people out there who desire what you have to offer. You just have to have the courage to seek them out. Once you sift through those who are not a good fit, you will have a better idea of who you are called to connect with and serve.

Let me share with you a story about when I did a Facebook Live video, and no one joined. I was extremely disappointed, but I kept going. I love the live interaction and feedback from my audience. So of course, I was wondering why I didn't have a single person join me. Well, when it was time to post my video, I realized that I had the settings on Only Me. This meant that there was no way that anyone could join because I never made my video public. This goes to show that errors can happen. Even when I discovered my error, my inner critic said, do not post this to Facebook, it will show you had zero viewers. But I posted it anyway, because someone needed to hear the message I delivered. Guess what? Your God-given assignment has nothing to do with how you feel. Sometimes you will feel embarrassed or even humiliated. Sometimes you will look at your number of followers, likes, and shares and wonder why people are not responding how you had imagined. We are responsible for sharing, but we are not supposed to be concerned about receiving praise and acknowledgment from others. Yes, it feels good, but what matters most is that you continue to share your gifts.

Contend For Your Promise

Did you know that opposition is confirmation you are on the right track? You cannot accomplish anything extraordinary without tenacity and endurance. Are you willing to be stretched? Some days you will probably ask yourself "what is going on?" It can feel like you have given your best, yet you are still far from where you feel like you should be. During these times you must immediately dismantle false statements that pop into your mind. Here are a few examples, you are a failure; You are not smart enough to do that; Nobody wants to marry you; Nobody wants to hire you; Look how long you've been waiting for _____.

Can I challenge you to become more in tune with what you say, what you think and what you come into agreement with? Now, you would rather sprint or better yet fly to your destination, but you will get to where you need to go, when it is your time to get there. So, instead of being discouraged, be encouraged. Do not waste time responding to unworthy distractions. Do what you can and hand the rest over to God. It's easier said than done, but you must pick yourself up and be happy, even when your circumstances are not going as planned. Tears of sorrow can become tears of joy. Your focus should be on what is in front of you, not on what is behind you. For your situation to change, you must first be willing to change perception of your situation.

Conquering Rejection

I have a long history with rejection. It is one of the areas requiring intentional effort on my behalf. I wish I had a magic formula for you, but I don't. However, what I have is confidence you can conquer rejection. I have confidence because the fear of rejection no longer orchestrates my life. What I have learned is that when you run from rejection, you are actually running from growth. Unfortunately, there is no way around rejection. You cannot force anyone to love and accept you. You cannot force an employer to hire you or a prospective client to do business with you. With that in mind, never measure your worth or value based upon the feedback you receive from others. You determine your value. Sometimes it takes a while for people to acknowledge your brilliance. Many times, people see you are talented, but they refuse to acknowledge it. Could it be that you were rejected, not because you were unqualified, but because you were aiming too low?

I had my first disturbing encounter with rejection in elementary school. As much as I tried to fit in, I just didn't. I wanted to be liked. I wanted to have a lot of friends, but I usually had only one or two friends. From there I felt rejected by my biological dad. He was in my life, but I never received the attention I desired. At this juncture of my life, my biological dad and I are closer than ever. God showed me that the anger and bitterness I had towards my biological father was preventing me from experiencing the freedom he desired for me to experience. If you are angry with anyone, I want you to understand that your peace is tied to your release. When you release those who have hurt you, rejected you or have caused you any emotional stresses, you will no longer be held captive by your emotions.

Besides experiencing rejection in secondary school and college, when I went into the workforce, guess what? Rejection followed me there too. It was like a dark shadow following me wherever I went. I kept thinking, God why can't I shake this? Rejected by family, rejected by colleagues, rejected by those I thought were my friends. Words cannot describe the pain associated with repeated rejection. When you have been hurt repeatedly, your natural response is to avoid that feeling at all costs. However, while trying to protect yourself, you build a wall and suppress your growth.

Have you ever tried to force a relationship that simply was not working? I have and it is like trying to squeeze a size nine foot into a size seven shoe. If we are honest with ourselves, some of our experiences resulted from pursuing people and positions not aligned with where God wanted to take us. Many goals that I pursued without first consulting with God ended up not working out. After experiencing hurt and frustration, I finally realized those relationships, ideas, jobs and so forth did not work out not because God had better plans. It felt like I was being punished, but God was actually trying to get something better to me. He was trying to get me to see that settling for "good enough" was not his plan for my life.

When you feel the nudge to make a change but you ignore it, this is when you experience turmoil. This is the period where you experience unprecedented disruption. Suddenly, the relationship that was rocky crumbles, the contract you were excited about somehow does not manifest, the layoff happens, you get fired and you did nothing wrong. If personal development is not a normal part of your life, these experiences can crush you. Your emotions will make you feel as though it is impossible for you to bounce back. Even if you are a confident person, repeated rejection can cause you to second guess yourself. Once you reach a place where you can experience rejection and keep pushing towards the mark, you will become unstoppable. The next time you experience rejection do not focus on what could have or should have occurred. Acknowledge your disappointment, allow yourself to vent and then pick yourself up and get back to work.

CHAPTER 5

Promotion Requires Preparation

Because you have made it this far, I am inclined to believe that you are committed to personal and professional growth. In this chapter, we will delve into promotion. Promotion is the term typically used to describe the act of being moved to a higher position or rank. While you will certainly learn what it takes to attain promotion, my primary focus will be centered on the process that takes place while you are on the path to promotion. It sometimes appears as though promotion is achieved quickly, but this is rarely the case. Why? Because a time of preparation always precedes promotion. In school, certain courses have prerequisites. There is a foundational course that must be taken first. Similarly, there are preconditions to promotion. Depending upon where you are, your season of preparation may be weeks, months or even years.

As you journey towards promotion, remain teachable and give yourself time to be properly equipped. Even if you are talented, you must learn from someone who has experienced success in the area where you desire to expand your influence. Also, never simply do what you are being asked to do. Always go above and beyond what is expected of you, because your "extra effort" is what will make you memorable. As a consultant, speaker and trainer, I consistently strive to over deliver. I over deliver when everything is going well and I over deliver when I am in a challenging situation. Regardless of how I feel, I am always seeking to figure out how I can over serve my clients. My goal is not to fit in, it is to stand out! The more you distinguish yourself, the more influential you will become. High achievers always give more and do more than what is expected of them. No, you cannot always control the actions of others. However, you can control your response.

So, even when you encounter a challenging personality, you should never lower the expectations you have established for yourself. Set the bar high and stay committed to the process.

Another element to remember is that you cannot rely on your network alone when seeking promotion. Now, your network is important. Who you are connected with influences your performance, your interests, and your beliefs. However, knowing the right people will not qualify you for a promotion. Your network can refer you, but if you are not adequately prepared, you cannot maintain your newly appointed position. Results matter. You might mislead people initially, but at some point, they will figure out that you cannot deliver on your promises. If you hope to be highly sought after, you must be extraordinary at what you do. You should consistently perform at a high level within your area of expertise. When your mind is set on promotion, you are willing to outwork, outstudy and outperform your competitors. There is a huge difference between being interested in promotion and being committed to it. When you get to a place where you will go above and beyond what is expected of you, you are committed to the process of promotion. Average people prefer to wait until an opportunity presents itself before they prepare, but those who are hungry for more in life prepare before the opportunity arrives. They already know what they would like to accomplish and they are increasing their knowledge, their skill, and their emotional intelligence levels now. With the right guidance, the right strategy and consistent preparation, you can reach your goals quicker and easier. However, you cannot bypass the process that accompanies promotion.

The Path to Promotion

The path to promotion is more of a winding road than a straight path. Often, we have our own idea of how we would like our vision to unfold. What happens is we create our personal timeline and we become frustrated when we encounter a detour. I know what it feels like to be waiting and waiting and wondering when it would finally be my turn to experience the joy promotion. I know what it feels like to see other people promoted and wonder why I am still stuck. I know what it's like to expend resources (money, time, energy) only to see little progress. However, what I have realized is that every challenge I encounter is preparing me for my forthcoming promotion. When you adopt this perspective, it is easier to remain calm when your life is not going as planned. Are you willing to become so laser-focused on achieving your vision, that you are no longer moved by attitudes, rejection or minor setbacks? As you grow, it is imperative that you're your ability to withstand pressure increases. Every challenge strengthens you and teaches you something that you did not know before. So, instead of running from challenges, view them as growth opportunities.

When you envision promotion in your mind, what does it look like? Does it look exhilarating? Does it look like a celebration with you and those closest to you? You will get to that point, but it takes time. We can see the finish line, but the middle is often a blur. Promotion requires patience and endurance because it often comes packaged in pain, disappointment and even adversity. Hence, you must make sure that you do not miss out on a breakthrough because it is not packaged how you have envisioned. It is imperative you do not deny a life-changing partnership because the person does not have the appearance, personality or background you prefer. If you are not careful, your preference can actually block your breakthrough. How often have you allowed someone's personality to push you away? Many times, I opted to run, simply because I did not want to deal with assertive personalities. I cannot ever recall feeling comfortable with confrontation. However, often, conflict is unavoidable. So, despite my natural inclination to head in the opposite direction, I must step back and figure out the most suitable way to resolve the conflict.

Embrace Discipline

Discipline is one word that will not make you feel all tingly inside. Just the word alone makes me cringe. I will not pretend that discipline flows easily for me. It is something that I must be intentional about daily. Sometimes I miss the mark and that is ok. Missing the mark does not give you permission to quit. Sometimes, you do not hit your target. Sometimes, you set your mind to do something, but you do the exact opposite. The key to victory is your willingness to get up, brush yourself off and go for it again. If you try it again and miss the mark, go for it again. You must repeat this cycle until you pass the test. Far too many people miss out on their breakthrough because they refuse to try again. The barrier to winning is usually not related to skill or ability. The barrier usually stems from giving up too soon.

Although I do not always want to be disciplined, it is the bridge between my desires and the attainment of my desires. For example, I had to be disciplined about writing and finishing this book. Did I encounter obstacles and challenges? Yes. Was I busy? Yes. Did I always FEEL like writing? No. Blocking off writing time required extreme discipline. It also required that I set a schedule and stick to it. Even with blocking the time off on my calendar, there would always be something that could replace my writing time. It was up to me to CHOOSE to write. Consistent discipline is the only remedy to procrastination. You must remain consistent, even when you do not feel like it.

You might struggle with self-doubt, feel overwhelmed, or you might be extremely frustrated. However, I encourage you to remain disciplined enough to stay the course. To get what you want, you must push through your inclination to do something easier. I have found it is best for me to complete the tasks I least enjoy first. I do this because the longer I procrastinate, the harder it becomes to tackle that task. The major difference between those who achieve their mission and those who don't is consistency and discipline. If you do what's difficult now, you can live easier later. Promotion will often require that you invest much more than you initially intended. Promotion requires risk. It also requires an exchange. Yes, you get something, but you are also required to give something in return. If you have difficulty following through on the commitments you have made to yourself or to others, I am challenging you to work on forming the habit of discipline.

Pursue Accountability

Accountability is the act of assuming responsibility for your action or inaction. Have you been holding yourself accountable? Have you set clear goals and clear action steps? Have you assessed your performance and productivity level? Accountability is a critical tool. By holding yourself accountable, you actually become more disciplined. Accountability has two spheres. One is holding yourself accountable. The other is finding someone else who will hold you accountable. You need both to perform at your highest level. I believe that everyone should have one or all of the following: a coach, a mentor, and/or an accountability partner. Think about it, actors, professional athletes, and singers have coaches and mentors. These are individuals who are considered gifted, yet they understand the importance of having someone to push them and hold them accountable. You should always have someone in your life who has been where you are attempting to go. You must be able to see that the goals you have set for yourself are not out of reach.

Far too often, we create barriers in our minds, and it takes an outsider to come in and show us we are not reaching our full potential. Do you have someone in your life that can see beyond the limitations you have set for yourself? Do you have someone who can see what you cannot see? Most people have gifts, talents, and skills locked inside of their inner vault. They have untapped potential and capacity. You will never know what is inside of you if you never challenge yourself. Using myself as an example, when I go to the gym, my visit is pretty bland. I may take a class, do a few crunches and get on the treadmill. This is ok, but it's definitely not my best. There are machines I will walk past because I feel as though I'm not at that level yet. However, when I am working with a personal trainer, he/she pushes me to do more. When I leave the gym, it is apparent that I have been working with a trainer. Likewise, when you have someone holding you accountable, you are more likely to push yourself beyond the glass ceiling you have created.

Now, when seeking an accountability partner, do not seek someone who will let you off easily and/or only tell what you want to hear. Jack Canfield once said that feedback is the breakfast of champions. I agree with this idea. Yes, feedback can make you uncomfortable and it might even hurt your feelings. However, feedback is the key to achieving better results the next time around. When working with my private coaching clients, at some point I must have a courageous conversation with them. Often, there is a fear, a habit or a limiting belief hindering their growth. In these moments, I must confront the elephant in the room. I do this out of love because my mission is to help them manifest their destiny. Your next dimension is contingent upon your willingness to be held accountable for the dream you have held on to for far too long. There is a time to dream, but there is also a time to manifest your dream.

Be Determined

On your path to promotion, determination is critical. It requires resolve, willpower and extreme focus. Determination also enables you to persist through challenges, obstacles and setbacks. How often have you been fired up about something and then you somehow got off track? Maybe you were distracted by another priority or your fire just fizzled out. This is why you must have a no matter what attitude about achieving your goals. Goal setting is easy, but goal getting takes work! Without determination, your chances of success are slim. Is determination all that you need? No, but it is a major piece of the puzzle. I am still in business, because I refused to give up, even when I REALLY wanted to. If I told you I never felt the urge to give up, I would be deceiving you. Much of my frustration resulted from not fully understanding the weight and the sacrifice of entrepreneurship. I have learned that the easy path is not necessarily the right path.

Are you willing to exchange temporary discomfort for long term happiness? I saw the glitz and glamour of creating my schedule and being my own boss. However, I did not realize that entrepreneurship requires more of you than any employer will require of you. As a leader, you must have staying power. You cannot retreat when you encounter an obstacle. When you are determined, you keep pushing, even when you experience rejection after rejection. Everyone can be in good spirits when they cross the finish line. However, the test is how you handle the dark moments. The true test is how you respond when you feel tired, frustrated and ready to throw in the towel. It is not in moments of celebration, but moments of tribulation when you determine whether you will achieve the big goal you have set for yourself. If you have not already, you are likely to have at least one meltdown where you question whether your dream is worth the investment. From experience, I can say with confidence, that your dream is worth the sacrifices you have made. Guess what, with every level, more will be required of you. The tests will continue to come, but you are equipped to pass them. You cannot claim to be a master of anything without completing an assessment. Just like you, I have not reached my final destination. I have not experienced a fraction of what is in store for me and neither have you!

Champions Train Differently

You are a champion and therefore you must train differently. Playing at the pro level requires a different dimension of commitment. You must stand still when you really want to run. There will be challenges that scare you. Sometimes, you must watch others obtain what you have been praying for. Do not view these situations as a punishment. You are just getting a glimpse of what you will experience if you remain faithful. Some people abandon their seed when it doesn't produce within the time frame they have set. Remember, when you sow a seed, you must cultivate it, nurture it, and protect it. Give your seed time to blossom.

Finally, the process of promotion will likely require that you appropriately manage a supporting role first. Would you be willing to work just as hard while in the supporting position as you would in the lead position? If you are supporting or being mentored by someone who has accomplished what you strive to accomplish, do not take this lightly. Often, you will intentionally be given the runner up position, just to see how well you accept it and how well you perform. This is not the time to be offended, jealous or bitter. This is the time to serve and learn. Whatever you do, do not despise your training ground. Instead of complaining, push harder. Yes, you deserve better and better is coming, but you must also be willing to celebrate the person currently in the number one position, even if you feel it should be you. Training precedes elevation. Don't run away from what frustrates you. Obstacles pave the way to extraordinary breakthrough. The idea of promotion is quite enticing, but you must be willing to withstand temporary discomfort. Continue to discover and refine your gifts. As you keep pushing, you will discover just how brilliant and powerful you are. I know the power of enduring and following through. You have come too far to stop now. Those who commit to crossing the finish line, will get to experience what it feels like to hold the gold medal.

The Growth Process

1. The Crushing Place- Extreme discomfort. Feeling broken. Season of uncertainty. Future Appears Dim.
2. Re-building Phase- life is better, but you're still not out of the woods. You still must fight to stay in the race.
3. Power Stride- This is where you catch on. You realize that you can do this. You feel a rhythm. You have obstacles, but you are in such a zone you are confident that you are equipped to overcome them.
4. Comfort Zone- The pressure and discomfort you initially experienced has lifted. If nothing changed, you would be ok. You have mastered your current level.
5. Repeat

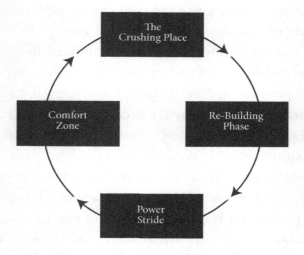

CHAPTER 6

Manifesting Your Vision

I n this chapter, you will learn what it takes to design and manifest your vision. The term manifest is defined as readily perceived by the eye. This means that when you manifest your vision, it transitions from simply being words on a sheet of paper or computer screen to becoming your reality. As you develop your vision, it is vital that you are specific. The key to setting great goals is having a specific target. This is important, because your mind has difficulty processing a general goal like, "I want to start a business" or "I want to lose weight." Furthermore, when your goal is specific, you are able to measure your progress or lack of progress. When establishing goals, you must know exactly what you want to accomplish. Although it can be difficult to pinpoint how much of a commitment your vision will require, you should never set a goal without creating a plan. The first section of this chapter will be laser focused on ensuring that you have clarity. I know that you are excited and passionate about manifesting your vision. However, I am asking that you contain it momentarily. Right now, your next step is to slow down and get clear. I will focus on entrepreneurship a great deal, because I believe that everyone should have multiple streams of income. However, even if entrepreneurship is not your goal, you will still gain a wealth of information from this chapter. For maximum value, you will need to take the time to answer the questions. But most importantly, you must be willing to do the work. Are you ready? Let's do this!

Slow Down and Get Clear

It is a very fulfilling and rewarding experience to coach aspiring and emerging entrepreneurs. I love helping my clients profit from their brilliance™ but getting clear is always the starting point. I wish I could say that a great idea and passion are all you need to have a profitable business. However, by doing so, I would be deceiving you. The truth is that entrepreneurship is quite complex. For this reason, you should never jump into any type of business without taking some time to get clear about what you would like your business to look like and how you plan to get there. Slowing down and getting clear will save you time and money. Trust me, clarity produces profits! Even, if you are considering a franchise or an MLM (Multi Level Marketing Company), you should not make a quick decision about forming a partnership. Starting a business will require a financial investment and you do not want to throw away your hard-earned money. Unfortunately, I had to learn this the hard way. If your goal is to experience consistent growth, you must take the time to build a solid foundation. So, while passion is a great inspirational tool, it does not guarantee sustainability or profitability.

Unfortunately, there are individuals who teach myths like "your passion will sustain you" or "build it (brand, product) and they will come." Yes, it sounds exciting. It might even motivate you to start a business, but If you accept these statements as valid, you are setting yourself up for a huge disappointment. Passion is an emotion and you have already learned that you should never make important decisions based upon your emotions. Your emotions change from day to day and sometimes from moment to moment. For this reason, I recommend that you never make a business decision based upon how you feel. I believe that you should always be guided by several factors including your gut (spirit, intuition), your intellect and research. Also, before making a commitment, make sure that you are not saying "Yes" out of guilt or because you feel pressured.

As you prepare to delve into formulating your vision, make sure that you declutter. When you declutter your mind and your personal space, you are creating an environment that is conducive to innovative thinking. I can tell you from personal experience that creativity cannot flourish in chaos. I recommend that you identify and remove any negative thinking patterns or distractions. This is not the time to think about what is not going right in your life. You might have to play some inspirational music or watch an inspirational video to ensure that you have the right frame of mind. Once your mind is clear, you are ready to create! There is a term called market research that you should become familiar with during the planning phase. It will help you become familiar with your market of choice and what is trending. By conducting market research, you will also be able to identify the individuals who are considered the elite in your industry. I recommend that you take note of the top 5 performers in your industry and study them. Why? Because they have a system in place that has helped them to become successful. You will want to see what angle they are taking and try to figure out how you can improve upon what they are already doing. The other option is to create a new product/service that meets a need that they are not currently addressing.

There are so many pieces to the puzzle of entrepreneurship that it can and sometimes will overwhelm you. Take a moment and answer the following questions: what topics do you enjoy talking about or learning about the most? What do people often ask you for advice about? Who can you connect with that is already doing what you desire to do? There are six areas that you want to master as a business owner. Leadership, Communication, Marketing, Sales, Operations and Finances. However, before you even begin studying these areas, you must identify your business type, your business structure, your business name, your target market, your target audience and your ideal client. I know that it is a lot to take in, but plan on setting aside ample time to study each of the aforementioned areas. Other questions to consider: Why do you desire to start a business? How long will it take you to get your business up and running? What resources will you need?

In essence, you do not want to jump into business and then try to figure out the foundational components. It is also essential that you commit to cultivating your knowledge base and skill set on a continual basis. Before anyone will do business with you, they must see the value that your product and/or service will provide. You must be able to clearly show them how you can solve their problem. You must also be able to prove that you can give them what they want. Experience has taught me that buyers are often more willing to invest in what they want before investing in what they need. This is why it is your duty and obligation to find out what they want and deliver it to them.

Research is important, because you are likely to waste time and money if you delve into creating a product or service based upon what you think. Far too many people spend time creating products and services that are not based upon research. Even if you have a great idea, it must be something that a person or an organization is willing to purchase. You might be wondering well how can I avoid this pitfall? The simple answer is to become an expert and an authority in your area of expertise. Ask questions, send surveys, review data, read books. Also, be willing to go a different route if you discover that people are not willing to pay for the product or service that you desire to create. Your family and friends will support you because they love you, but everyone else must be convinced that your product/service is worth their investment.

Upgrade Your Vision

As you develop your vision, it is also important that you revamp your perception of what you can and cannot accomplish. During the planning phase, you will be inclined to set goals based upon how you currently view yourself. While this seems logical, it actually diminishes your ability to increase your capacity. At this juncture, I am challenging you to start seeing yourself in a new way. I want you to form a vision that will take some time for you to grow into. During this phase, you should not be concerned about resources. Never downsize your vision to align with the resources that you have right now. If you will commit to pursuing your vision, provision will be made at the right time. A vision that is easily attainable is not a vision, because it does not challenge you. I believe that many of us have been guilty of "playing small" more often than we would care to admit. Have you ever decided not to express what you really wanted, because you were afraid that you would not be able to obtain it? When you do this, you cheat yourself out of a growth opportunity. Every significant achievement requires significant effort. Are you willing to upgrade your belief about what your life will look like in 3-5 years? If you commit to manifesting your vision, in 3-5 years, everything about you will be different. You deserve to have a vision that stretches you. Do not worry about seeming unrealistic. If you want to create an exceptional lifestyle, you must first have an exceptional vision.

Upgrading your vision, requires that you challenge your self-doubt and silence your inner critic. Just take a moment and imagine what you could accomplish over the next 12 months if you would just commit to challenging yourself more. Imagine what you could accomplish if you would commit to taking imperfect action. At first glance, perfectionism seems harmless. However, if you leave it unchecked, it will lock you out of your purpose. Perfection is not what you should strive for, because it produces procrastination and fear. What you should strive for is excellence. Yes, you always want to put forth your best effort. However, perfectionists often struggle with creating, because they are rarely satisfied with their best effort. As a recovering perfectionist, I know that there is a point when I just have to let go and release the product/service. If I did not contain myself, I could work on this book for years. When you are a perfectionist, 80-90 percent is your launch goal. In other words, do not hold on to your project until you are 100 percent satisfied. I do not want you to be so obsessed with being perfect that you never get the courage to share the brilliance that is within you. Remember, it is better to try and miss the mark, than not try at all. I want you to get acquainted with feeling uncomfortable. You have the power to transform your feelings of anxiety and hesitation into energy and excitement. We are naturally wired to avoid discomfort. However, instead of retreating, be intentional about pushing yourself out of your comfort zone. Take bold action and begin declaring what it is that you will accomplish over the next 12 months. Now, ask yourself how you can stretch that goal. Okay, you have done the preliminary work. There is no turning back!

Tap into Your Brilliance

Now that you have upgraded your vision, you are ready to tap into your brilliance. This is the phase where you begin to utilize the brilliance that has likely been held captive for far too long. (Your Name) there is someone somewhere waiting for you to tap into your brilliance, so that they can begin walking in their destiny. Guess what? The longer you wait, the longer they have to wait. Greater is calling you and this is your season to answer. I truly hope that you are willing to stay focused, even when it seems like you have been waiting on your moment FOREVER. A lot of people get discouraged when they see just how tough it is to become the person that they have dreamed of becoming. Visionary, you can't choose to throw in the towel just because your phone is not ringing. You can't decide to quit because you are not getting the opportunities that you know you deserve. Everyone who has ever made a major accomplishment has been right where you are right now. In fact, there were several instances where I was not just disappointed, I was beyond frustrated. I was doing the work, but people did not seem to notice my brilliance. It almost seemed as if I was invisible.

Do you know what the turning point for my business was? The turning point was when I shifted my thought processes. I decided that I was obligated to carry the weight of getting me noticed. Yes, I did want the invitations, phone calls and emails, but waiting for them was not working. I had financial goals and being idle caused more pain than the pain of rejection. So, I decided that I would I would come face to face with my fear of rejection. I had reached a point where I had to go after the very thing that had chased me since childhood. Setting myself up to be rejected was my only way of escape. This meant that I had to stop sitting around waiting for others to recognize my brilliance. This meant that I had to pursue clients. Did you know that rejection typically precedes selection? Once you reach a certain level in business, prospective clients will begin to seek you out. However, the first few years will require that you take on the uncomfortable task of asking people to hire you and/or purchase your products and services. Once you discover how valuable you are, you will not waste another day waiting for someone to choose you, you will choose yourself. You will declare what your destiny holds and pursue it like you have never pursued it before.

When feelings of fear or inadequacy try to consume your thoughts, you must counteract them with the truth. Assess what you have and recognize what you hold. When you are fully aware of your strengths, your gifts and your skills, you can remind yourself that you are equipped for your current assignment. In addition to writing down what you know, you should also seek to discover the gifts, talents and skills that you have not tapped into yet. Below, I have outlined the steps that (if followed) will lead you to your sphere(s) of influence.

Step 1. *Identify Your Genius:* What is it that you have excelled at since childhood? What are your top 3 skills? For example, are you a great writer, communicator, teacher, photographer, organizer, etc. What comes easy to you, but is sometimes perceived as difficult or cumbersome for others? What area(s) are you extraordinarily gifted in (health, finances, relationships, spirituality, design, business, technology)? When you master something, you are equipped to teach in that area.

Step 2. *Analyze and Select:* Based upon your area(s) of interest, your skill set and your knowledge base, what can you teach others? This is where you can begin teaching others something that you already know. Basically, because of your depth of knowledge, you are considered an expert in this area. Who is looking for support in this area?

Step 3. *Establish Your Foundation:* Get clear on what you will offer. Now that you know your sphere of influence, I need you to get clear on the type of transformation that potential clients will receive as a result of working with you. The next thing you will need to do is identify your target audience and your ideal client. Who would you enjoy servicing, coaching and or training? A prospective client should know without a doubt that you are the solution to their challenge.

Step 4. *Create a Profitable Product:* Based upon your gifts, talents and skills, identify three ways you can begin generating cash. Ex. Write a book, work part-time as an instructor or consultant, create a virtual coaching program, etc. Perhaps, you prefer to provide a service like catering, organizing or caregiving. The goal is for you to put your brilliance to work.

By doing so, you will access a level of wisdom and ideas that you were not aware of before. You have ideas and skills that will open doors and create amazing opportunities for you.

Take Confident Action

Your vision will require confident action. Taking confident action is the point where you stop saying what you would like to do and start taking steps towards your goal using what you already have. Over analyzing and indecision is not allowed at this level. You have talked, you have researched and you have gotten clarity. Now it is time for you to move from desire to action. You can't just want to eat, you must be hungry. When you are hungry, you do not shut down after receiving a string of rejections. When you are hungry "No" will actually fuel you. Of course, no one really wants to receive or deal with rejection. The key is to never attach how you feel to what you do. When your effort is based upon how you feel, your performance is not reliable. For example, you can be having a very productive day, but then you receive a negative email, text message or performance review and you decide that you no longer feel like working. You start thinking that what is happening to you is unfair and you are probably correct. However, what happens is, you get so deep in self-pity that you feel the urge to take the rest of the day off and just pick up where you left off when you feel better. Well, this does not seem all that bad, until it becomes a habit. Do you realize how much time you are losing when you choose to let your emotions win? Succumbing to your feelings is a sure way to delay your progress. In fact, if this becomes how you handle challenges, you will always find yourself trying to make up for lost time. If you are serious about manifesting your vision, you must put forth your best effort, even when you are not in the best mood. Performing at a high level, requires that you never lose sight of your vision. Whenever you notice that you are not putting forth your best effort, call yourself out. Even when it appears to others that you are doing a great job, you know when you are slacking.

There are times when life will throw you a curve ball that makes you feel as though you are just plain unlucky. You might be saying to yourself, I'm a nice person, I don't steal, I am always willing to lend others a helping hand, so why aren't things working in my favor? Well, I have certainly been there. In fact, I have had some days when I didn't think that I had another tear left to cry. I literally wanted to run away from my life. I was tired of getting my hopes up, just to be let down again. It actually seemed more reasonable to quit than to keep going. Had I quit when I felt like quitting, this book never would have been written. Yes, there will be unexpected twists and turns, but I am confident that you are an overcomer. Your ability to persist is contingent upon how you think and what you say to yourself about yourself. You must control your mind, you cannot let it control you. So, when a negative thought enters your mind, ask yourself if that particular thought will take you down a path of confidence and hope or down a path of self-doubt and fear. My hope is that you will immediately dismantle the negative chatter that we all battle. It is time for you to buckle down and work your plan. In the bold action phase, you are building and nurturing your vision. What do you need to take action on today? Your vision won't manifest out of thin air, you must put in the work. Your vision requires, focus, execution, patience and persistence. You have a destiny to fulfill, so get focused and take bold action.

Contend for Your Vision

By now, you understand that your vision will not be like taking a refreshing walk in the park. Growth is never comfortable. During this journey you will be challenged, pulled and stretched. This is why you must have mental toughness. In addition to mental toughness, you must have patience and the right strategy. You cannot get to your next dimension of health, wealth, relationships, business or ministry if you are not willing to be uncomfortable. The great news is that the discomfort is only temporary. That place of discomfort is preparing you for the challenges that you will encounter once you begin to soar higher. So, step up to the challenge, knowing that your temporary discomfort will ultimately produce a long-term benefit. Now do you understand why your vision must be clear and specific? You must know without a doubt what you will produce as a result of the sacrifices that you will have to make. You can't pick and choose which part of this process you would like to get involved with. It is all or nothing. You must get clear, you must tap into your brilliance, you must upgrade your vision, you must take bold action and you must contend. Anything worth having is worth fighting for.

When you are under pressure, remind yourself that elevation doesn't just happen. You must trust the process. Vision boards are great, I have several vision boards. However, a vision board without a strategy is just a wish. You must create a goal and strategy that will get you from where you are to where you desire to be. I can remember reading books about how you can just think yourself into where you desire to be. That was exciting, because there was very little required of me. But, I soon realized that imagining a new home, a larger bank account and so forth was just the starting point. You can and should imagine (paint a vivid picture of) what you desire, but if you are not willing to work for it, you probably don't want it bad enough. Let your desire for a better life push you into your destiny. Let it pick you up during those moments when you are not as excited as you were during the idea phase. You cannot break through if you don't have anything to break through. Don't just say "I want to manifest my vision," pursue it with everything you've got. Each level will require more of you. Keep learning, keep growing and keep pressing. I want to be a part of your journey. Please reach out to me and let me know how you are progressing using the strategies outlined in this chapter. You can connect with me by visiting http://expectingvictory.com/

The Path to Victory

Even if it does not feel like it, you are on the path to victory. Everything that you have experienced up until this point has prepared you for where you are heading. We all desire to be victorious. However, desire is not enough to carry anyone across the finish line. To be victorious, you must do what it takes to experience a victory. Your journey will have highs and lows. It will often feel like you are in a boxing match because you really are in a fight. You are fighting for your vision, your peace, and your legacy. It is important that you commit to being a good steward over your focus and your energy. As you have learned in previous chapters, your victory will be not be handed to you. So, if you get knocked down, you must get back up. One thing I know for sure, you have the power to get back up. You are not defeated unless you quit. As you pursue your victory, I am right there with you, cheering you on.

Release to Breakthrough

If I asked you would you like a supernatural breakthrough in the area of your life that challenges you the most, your response would likely be an astounding "YES." In fact, you might even go to the extent of responding with "who wouldn't want a breakthrough." If you have been pursuing a particular goal for months or even years, your breakthrough probably seems well overdue. As much as we all love breakthroughs you must be positioned to receive your breakthrough. We are now in an era of extreme busyness. If you are not careful, your life can become filled with so many tasks you barely have time to truly enjoy life. When you are in a state of doing too much, you become overwhelmed, you become anxious and you actually decrease your level of productivity. In the previous chapter, we talked about the importance of getting clear, so you can ultimately manifest your destiny. In this chapter, I really want you to think about what is serving you well, what can be repaired and what must be released. Your breakthrough will require an honest self-assessment. On a scale of 1-10, rate your health (mental, emotional, physical), relationships, finances, and professional achievement. Are you doing all that you can to achieve the breakthrough you have been seeking? Your actions must align with what you say you want. This means that unhealthy relationships, habits, and/or thought patterns must be identified and released.

When you have too many obligations, it becomes difficult to focus on what matters most. If you are not laser focused, it is easy to become distracted by people and tasks not in sync with your goals. Usually an insignificant task will start as a small detour. However, before you know it, you have wasted several hours of your time on a trivial task. It could be watching television, going to the movies, cleaning out your email inbox or surfing social media. I am not saying you should avoid the items listed, but you must place time limits on them. Performing at a high level requires a high level of sacrifice. This means you must release all of your breakthrough blockers. I have a question for you, are you able to identify the people and habits that have been slowing or halting your growth? Are you willing to take the time to identify and fix the leaks in your mindset and your performance? When you go to your physician regarding a symptom you are experiencing, he/she can sometimes identify and correct the issue based upon your description. However, sometimes, your physician must dig a little deeper, by running tests or recommending that you visit a specialist.

Likewise, you must dig a little deeper. You must go beyond the surface to discover what has been preventing you from experiencing the breakthrough you have been longing for.

Shut Down Your Inclination to Worry

Despite what you come up against, you get to choose what you think about, how you spend your time and where you exert your energy. This means, that you have the power to think yourself into or out of a state of anxiety. When you are in despair, you weaken your ability to fight for your breakthrough. Worry distracts you and causes you to lose focus. Worry diminishes your hope and stirs up unbelief. This is why you must be intentional about shutting down your natural inclination to worry. You must war against the voice constantly reminding you of your circumstances. Now, I am not saying you should ignore your problems. Awareness and acknowledgment are key to the problem-solving process. However, constantly focusing on your problems will likely send you into a downward spiral. What happens is you play the same broken record and end up feeling burdened, stressed and anxious. When challenges arise, instead of reactive sinking (anxiety), which is a common response, I am challenging you to go into strategic thinking mode You have two options, you can focus on your obstacles or you can focus on how to overcome your obstacles. One will burden you and one will free you. The great news is that you get to choose.

Your focus is pivotal, because it determines how you feel and it ultimately determines your quality of life. Let me give you a simple strategy that works. When you feel like you are sinking into a state of anxiety, you must change your internal station from pity to praise. So, instead of crying about what you are lacking, express gratitude for what you have right now. Even if everything seems to spin out of control, I am sure that you have something to be grateful for. What weight do you need to release at this moment? Worry and doubt weakens the glue that bonds the promises of God. I want you to declare that you are free from worry and anxiety. You were not placed on this earth to simply exist. I do not want you to just APPEAR to be confident and happy, I want you to actually EXPERIENCE IT! When worried, your mind is like a congested highway, you are barely moving and you feel stuck. What if instead of worrying, you started working? Will you commit to replacing the habit of worrying with the habit of building? I cannot say this enough, do not be discouraged by the refining process. Your final script has not been written. I am challenging you to recognize the winner inside of you. Once you set your mind on winning, you are positioned for victory.

Keys to Abundant Living

Abundance is defined as having a very large quantity of something. We often link abundance to finances, but abundance can be related to other areas of your life as well. For example, you can experience abundance related to your level of creativity, your outlook, relationships, health and much more. If you are not seeing the results you desire to see, you might benefit from investing in inner work. Inner work is a key component of self-growth. Sometimes the issue blocking your breakthrough appears to be external, but it is actually internal. For example, there may be feelings of hopelessness, pain or even anger that have been suppressed for years. By not looking internally, you can without realizing it, miss out on a life-changing opportunity. Have you ever passed up an opportunity, because, in your mind, you were not qualified to pursue it? As your virtual coach, I'm asking you, what is really holding you back? Is it a person? Is it a habit? Is it fear of the unknown? Is it self-doubt? If you have been struggling financially. Consider some of these questions. What are your attitudes, beliefs, and feelings about money? What do you think about wealthy people?

I can remember dealing with infertility and being extremely jealous of pregnant women. I would become angry and complain about how unfair it was that I had difficulty conceiving. But, after having two meltdowns in front of my mom, she told me that I cannot have anything that I despise. I initially did not want to hear what she had to say, because after all, she is a mother of three. In my mind, she couldn't possibly understand what it felt like to desire to be a mom and not be able to make that desire a reality. However, after calming my emotions, I realized that she was right. I asked God to forgive me and I celebrated friends and family members who told me they were pregnant. Guess what? Not long after that process, I became pregnant. So, to bring this back to wealth, if you have an issue with wealthy people, you might really want to be wealthy, but you must first deal with your internal perception of wealthy people. This is important because if you think that wealthy people are selfish or greedy, why would you want to become wealthy? The thoughts you have about wealthy people might have stemmed from your upbringing or something that you heard your parents say about wealthy people when you were a child.

After doing some inner work, I realized that I had to reframe my thoughts about money and wealth. My feelings about money were evident every time I had to negotiate a salary or set fees because I would consistently short change myself. I also felt guilty about having extra money in my bank account, knowing I had family members and friends struggling financially. So, what did I do? I would take people (friends, family colleagues) out to eat, on trips or simply let people borrow large sums of money, knowing I would never get it back. My guilt prevented me from living abundantly. Have you ever taken less than you deserved, because you did not want to be perceived as greedy or selfish? I have. If you have not given yourself permission to live abundantly, take the time to do it now. You have only to declare these words: I give myself permission to be wealthy! It may seem a little weird, but trust me on this one. The simple act of giving yourself permission to be wealthy will remove the padlock you have unknowingly placed on the door to wealth.

Since childhood, I have been bombarded with many negative perceptions about money and wealthy people. Also, because my family struggled, I always believed that money was scarce. Even after graduating from college and earning a comfortable salary, my beliefs about money followed me. I would stock up on simple household items, because I feared running out. I had experienced being in a place of "not enough" and did not want to ever experience it again. So, all of my experiences with money directly affected my perception of wealth. Have you ever heard statements like "wealthy people are unhappy, lonely, selfish, and so forth?" If so, whether you know it or not, those thoughts have been planted in your subconscious mind. The subconscious is the part of the mind you may not fully know of, but it influences your actions and feelings. I now have a better understanding of how my beliefs about money are directly correlated to my bank account balance. To shift my thinking patterns, I had to confront my faulty mental narrative and acknowledge that it was wrong. By shifting your thoughts around money, you are positioning yourself for abundant living.

Boldly Unleash Your Gifts

Are you ready to stop hiding out and start stepping out? If so, I am challenging you to boldly unleash your gifts. In the previous chapter, you identified your genius and figured out where you are most gifted. Now, you must cultivate your gifts and skills. Your path to victory will require a level of boldness that you may not be familiar with. Some people may be intimidated by your boldness. Some people may be offended by your boldness. However, those who are intimidated or offended are not the people that you have been called to impact. You cannot expect other people to believe in your brand, your products and/or your services if you don't. Now, I'm not advising you to be arrogant. Arrogance is when you have a sense of superiority and pride. However, confidence is self-assurance and belief in your abilities. If you are timid or shy, no worries because confidence and boldness are skills. You do not have to be born with these traits, they can be learned.

I discovered early on that I was pretty good at writing, listening and helping people. However, I basically remained in my comfort zone and I was afraid to try tasks that did not come easily. Some of this was related to my perfectionism. I was never a really competitive person, but I always desired to do well. I always had a desire to be at the top of my class, go to college and I did those things. However, my limited perception of what I could accomplish actually held me back. I was trained as a social worker, but there were so many other gifts, talents, and skills that low self-confidence prevented me from tapping into. Many gifts and talents I am operating in today took years for me to discover. Many of my gifts were revealed through coaching, prayer and my willingness to step out and try something new. As a result of stretching myself, I discovered that I was a great teacher, trainer, speaker, coach and much more. I did not discover all of my gifts at once. It was layered because I would have to break through the chatter in my mind telling me that I was not qualified or equipped.

Skills are learned, but gifts are given. So, your gifts are already inside of you. It's just your job to tap into them. How much time and energy have you invested in identifying and cultivating your gifts? Helpers and givers are notorious for helping everyone else, but when it comes to their dreams, they are placed on the back burner until they find enough time. Do you know of any professional athletes who do not schedule time to train and practice? Of course not. Just because they are among the elite, that does not mean there is no room for growth. Likewise, you should schedule time to invest in your growth and development. I want you to train like an athlete would train for an Olympic medal. I'm sure that at some point they felt nervous about competing at such a high level. However, they were willing to invest whatever it took (ethically speaking) to improve their skill and their stamina. They had to work out when they were happy and work out when they were sad. They had to practice when they were full of energy and practice when they were drained. They had to get out of bed on sunny days and on rainy days. You cannot allow your circumstances to determine your level of commitment. When your path to victory gets tough remember that you are being prepared for the promotion YOU asked for. You don't have to be perfect, you just have to be committed.

CHAPTER 8

Get Ready to Soar

Congratulations, you have been commissioned to soar! You have been mandated to rise to a higher level. As we bring this journey of profitable conversations to a close, get ready to come up to a level of living you have not experienced before. Get ready to courageously step into your purpose. Your days of hesitating and second-guessing yourself are over. In this season, you must live outside of your comfort zone. Do not try to retreat back to your place(s) of comfort. Your place of comfort can be a previous career, relationship or way of living. During the moments when I seriously considered going back to my comfort zone, God asked me a powerful question. He said, of course, you can go back to being a school social worker. However, if you did, would you be happy? That question hit me like a ton of bricks. I was frustrated with this entrepreneurship roller coaster and I was ready to go back to having a set schedule and a set paycheck. I knew that my stress level would decrease dramatically. But I also knew that God had called me to do more.

Although I was ready to walk away from entrepreneurship, I knew without a doubt that I was called to do more than social work. I knew that I was being commissioned to utilize my gifts. However, I was basically allowing impatience to get the best of me. When you are halfway up the mountain, it is tempting to go back down, because continuing to climb will take some serious work. When frustrated with your current level of progress, you are likely to rationalize why it makes more sense to go back. A rough patch often makes what you walked away from APPEAR enticing, even if you were unfulfilled when you were there. Please do not get entangled in the slippery slope of impatience. Not wanting to wait any longer seems harmless, but it can ultimately cause you to settle for so much less than you deserve.

Now, even as you soar, life will not be perfect. You will encounter ground level distractions that will attempt to weigh you down. However, as an overcomer, you are guaranteed to bounce back. The trials you encounter will always seem overwhelming when viewed from ground level. You are not an imposter just because you fall into a slump occasionally. It happens to all of us. The key is to recognize your faulty thinking and remind yourself that you no longer live at ground level. You visit the ground level, but you live in another dimension. That dimension is the faith dimension. Just picture yourself on an airplane flying over cities that would look huge if you were on ground level. However, because of where you are seated, you can barely see them. Your perception changes in the faith dimension. As you ascend, your problems no longer overwhelm or consume you. It's not that you no longer care, you just choose not to be discouraged by what you see.

Finding Balance

A key to soaring is understanding the importance of moving and resting. Too much work and you become burned out. Too little work and you will become overwhelmed by the work that is piling up. Balance has been and will continue to be a popular topic of discussion, particularly among working women with families. I initially struggled with balance, because my goal was to distribute my time evenly. However, trial and error have helped me tremendously. I now have a more realistic definition of balance. I define balance as determining how to integrate all the moving pieces of your life. Balance should be rigid enough to keep you on track, but flexible enough to allow a detour when needed. For example, when travel requires that I stay away from home for a few days, it creates a detour from my regular schedule. Upon returning home, I step away from my computer (really tough) and schedule much-needed quality time with my family.

What works for me, may not work for you. This is why you must determine your work-rest intervals. There will be days of supernatural energy. There will be days when you can beat your deadlines and tackle every task on your to-do list. You might even feel like you can run a marathon. Those days are amazing. I wish I could tell you that you could have that experience every day. However, in doing so, I would be deceiving you. I have been at events where I was hyped and motivated, yet once reality set in, I was back to feeling lost and frustrated. What I want to ensure is that you have tools and strategies that will meet you where you are. Everyone can't afford a nanny, a private chef or an assistant. So, until you get to that place, use the time and energy you have wisely.

I love coffee, but at some point, the energy produced by caffeine will wear off. Because you are human, there will be moments when you simply feel the need to slow down and rest. Resting revitalizes you. Soaring does not mean you are always moving at an accelerated pace. When building muscle, you stretch it to its limit and then you allow it to rest. During its resting phase is when the muscle actually grows. So, while I want you to work and produce. I also want you to recognize that resting is just as important as grinding.

If you want to avoid crashing, please schedule time to rest. Besides increasing your energy, resting also sharpens your creativity and mental focus. By scheduling adequate rest, you make it easier to enter your place of flow. Your place of flow is your zone. It is the place where you have adequate rest, energy and mental focus. Ideally, you want to experience a state of flow daily even if it is only for a few hours. Life can get hectic, but self-care is not an optional task you find time for. It is imperative you create time to refresh your mind and body. Soaring requires disciplined working and disciplined resting.

Protect Your Progress

Soaring requires that you take authority over your mind and your emotions. I have emphasized mindset a great deal, because your mindset determines how far you will go. Even when you begin to see your dreams unfolding, you must continue to train your mind and your emotions to follow your lead. You will not always FEEL like soaring. Why? Because soaring means that you must always take the high road. For example, you cannot soar and be rude to someone, because they were rude to you (ouch). You cannot be easily upset or easily offended. Remember you are soaring, but some of the people you interact with have not reached your level of maturity. If those around you will not come up, you definitely should not be going down to their level. In doing so, you figuratively must step out of your realm, which is a higher realm.

Because you have been commissioned to soar, you must walk in love. You must forgive quickly. You cannot hold on to offense for years, months or even weeks. You must address the anger, disappointment and pain caused intentionally or unintentionally by someone else. You must also forgive yourself. We have all made mistakes we are not proud of. However, if you are not careful, a root of bitterness will be planted. When you harbor anger and bitterness, your heart becomes tainted. When your heart becomes tainted, it is difficult to enjoy life. Every time you feel good, your mind will go back to what happened and your joy will be disrupted. You cannot be happy and angry at the same time, you must choose one. Visionary, I do not want you to become too distracted to soar. If you are having trouble forgiving, forgive by faith and ask God to heal your heart and any wounds or trauma associated with the incident stealing your peace.

There are some who believe that forgiving is letting the other person off the hook. This is not the case. You forgive for you, not the perpetrator. If what they did was a criminal act, they should deal with the consequences. If you revisit a situation in your mind or in a discussion and you immediately feel angry, this indicates that you have more work to do in that area. The heaviness of unforgiveness will weigh you down. Being weighed down is counterproductive. The more you carry, the harder it becomes to soar.

Finish Strong

One of my favorite quotes is "It's not how you start out, it's how you finish." Getting started is great, but if you desire to move from dreaming your dream to living your dream, you must be a finisher. Finishers have endurance. Finishers can take a hit, get back up and pick up where they left off.

Crossing the finish line will require that you view success as a marathon and not a sprint. Sometimes, the issue is that you are trying to do too much too fast and you have now become distressed and burned out. You must pace yourself. It is also good to set aside time to assess your progress and make changes as needed.

I'm willing to bet that at some point you have watched others attain the very goal(s) that you have been pursuing. You've cried, you've prayed, you've wanted to give up. You've felt inadequate and overlooked, but despite what you've felt and despite what you have been up against, you kept going. You will only receive credit for what you finish. Because you have been commissioned to soar, you can't simply finish, you must finish strong!

Follow Dr. Houston on social media.

@DrJessHouston

Jessica Houston Enterprises

Dr. Jessica Houston

@DrJessHouston

Made in the USA
Columbia, SC
04 November 2024

45304814R00063